Words We Might One Day Say

For Courtney —
So excited to meet a fellow Arlington poet & to read your books!

Words We Might One Day Say

Holly Karapetkova

Washington Writers' Publishing House
Washington, D.C.

Copyright © 2010 by Holly Karapetkova. All rights reserved.

Printed in the United States of America by Lightning Source, Inc.

Library of Congress Cataloging-in-Publication Data

Karapetkova, Holly.
  Words we might one day say / by Holly Karapetkova.
    p. cm.
  ISBN 978-0-931846-95-3
  I. Title.
  PS3611.A74W67 2010
  811'.6—dc22

                                2010014483

Washington Writers' Publishing House
P.O. Box 15271,
Washington, DC 20003
www.washingtonwriters.org
wwphpress@gmail.com

For Peter

Contents

I.
The Woman Who Wanted a Child *3*
Mara and the Hen *4*
Sorrow and the Empty Sac *6*
Love Poem *7*
Synsethete *8*
Lessons in Kindness *9*
Once Upon a Time in the West *10*
Parts of Speech *11*
After We Called It Quits *12*
That Kind *13*
For My American Lover, Upon My Leaving *14*
Sofia in April, 1997 *15*
Atlas *16*
Leaving the Dig *17*
A Fairy Tale *18*
Portrait: Girl at 19 *19*
Stolen Child *20*
The Lost Mommy *21*

II.
Letter in Response to a Friend's Suicide Note *25*
Street Dogs *26*
A Confession *27*
The One That Got Away *28*
Entropy *29*
Cadaver Room *30*
Grandmother's Machine *31*
Grandfather and Dog *32*
Love and the National Defense *33*
A Personal History *34*
Democracy Comes to the Black Sea *35*

Deserts at Night   *36*
Postcards from the Field   *37*
Playing the Rain   *38*

III.
Wild Child   *43*
First Child   *44*
Learning the Language   *45*
At the Window   *47*
Before Language   *48*
At Eight Months   *49*
First Words   *50*
After Breakfast   *51*
Late Afternoon   *52*
How the Earth Lost Its Moon   *53*
Art Lesson   *55*
Clothes for Iraqi Orphans   *56*
Housing Nationalization   *58*
Dinner With Foreigners   *59*
End of Myth   *61*
The Girl with the Sheep's Heart   *62*
The Cult of True Womanhood   *63*
The Orchard Grower's Wife   *64*
Refugees   *65*
The Fifth War   *66*

Notes
Acknowledgments
About the Author
Colophon

I.

The Woman Who Wanted a Child

For a short time I walked the earth as a woman, breathed in the scent of gardenias and gasoline, made love to a man. We lived in a small house with a narrow staircase leading upwards into nothing; the second floor was never built. I fed him fresh garlic and parsley from our garden, the smell rising to the top of the staircase where we made love, knees and ribcages bumping against the ceiling. But my throat grew dry, my feet stuck in the dust. At night, while he slept, I walked down to the marsh where the birds gathered to dive for fish, the water wetting my waterless lips, the gentle rocking soothing the aches in my feet, my arms. Please, I said to the white tern bringing her six little hatchlings bits of fish guts, you a mother who has so many children, help me a mother who has none.

The next morning, I woke up vomiting feathers. In a few months, my belly was round and full as a blowfish and I felt the flutter against my ribcage. I walked down to the banks of the marsh, spread my legs, and out she came, a pure royal tern, her white feathers beaded with blood. She was hungry and I had nothing to give her; she would not take my milk. I waded out to find the mother bird on the other side of the marsh. I cannot help you, she said, I have my own children to feed. So I turned into a fish. My daughter dove, grasped me in her beak, and swallowed me whole. Now, I live within her light body. We spend our days upon the high winds, bumping only against the sky. Now, I feed her.

Mara and the Hen

The hen pecks at the dust,
she pecks at a rock,
there is nothing to eat,
she's the last one left.
Mara snaps at her,
do something useful with yourself.
The hen stares back,
what else should I do?
Mara draws green water up
from the well, heavy with sludge.
She no longer boils it, waits
for it to settle.

Clouds form, pass by, taking rain
somewhere else.
She has watched everything
dry up and die,
cracking the stale grains
between her teeth.

She thinks of her children
whose souls have gone elsewhere.
She always thought
they would come back
lightened of their bodies
and play in the yard.
She thinks of the child
growing inside her
floating in a tub of murky water,
eyes closed, tail of a fish.
It will not live long.
There will be no milk,
like with the others,
only a few drops of blood
bitter, dripping from her nipples.

Once she loved a man
who got drunk on vodka
made from tomato paste
thick as dried blood.
He stumbled into the yard
and shot her chickens
one by one,
all but the last hen
who has nothing to eat
and will not lay eggs.
Stop! she snaps at the hen,
there's nothing left here!
She sees the new baby
pecking at her dry breast,
its small mouth opening
and closing, opening.

Sorrow and the Empty Sac

Sorrow came down from her mountain
with the tears that melt into rivers of tears:
Why do you not keep me company? she asked.
Why do you not let me in?
You've been spending too much time
with happiness, my heedless twin.
Then she took my child growing inside,
planted it up on the mountain
and handed me the empty sac.

The summer rains came, flooding
through the house I had worked so hard
to prepare, the small socks for mockingbirds,
the bed of fresh pine with its knotted elbows,
vases clotted with mud, heaving
with the pain of swallowing so much pain.

Happiness hid behind the stove whispering
promises, come out to the yard and see.
From beneath the ground my child's eyes
stretched up into rivers, her mouth the scream
of a wind, her hair a willow tree.
Nothing more.

When sorrow came down from the mountain
with the first snow of winter on her back
this time I called her name.
This time I called her in.

Love Poem

It was you who finally found
the glasses I couldn't see without
but had carelessly left
in some unmemorable spot,
folded neatly into empty oblong eyes.
I was annoyed by the ease of your discovery.

And there were other signs:
the first rain in three months
fell steadily on the day you arrived
and for three days after,
the tightly clinched sky
finally splitting, spilling over.

Then, the brown creeper
that flew in our open window.
I flinched,
remembering the thud
when a wren entered my childhood home
and slammed against the glass,
the tiny trickle of blood
that slipped down its beak—
but you, reaching out
toward the frenzied blur of brown and white,
grasped without crushing,
spoke comfortingly in an odd falsetto
until I dared to look up,
to watch it flutter into open air
and breathe.

Synesthete

Peppermint tastes like a frozen lake,
smooth and cold beneath skates;
chocolate, white cows on a bright green field.
The letter "L" is pink and *anger*
purple, the color glowing with the word
on the page, around its sound in the air.

I was ten before I realized what I was.
I told my reading teacher
the girl in the story saw not envy
but embarrassment when she saw green.
The teacher stared at me blankly
and sent me to the school counselor.

After that, I grew careful.
When I fell in love with the boy
whose kiss made clouds spin out
like peacock feathers against the sky,
whose name was cherry red, my favorite color,
who swelled around me in a hum

like a swarm of bees, like the sense
of flying across a field of lavender
on a horse going faster and faster;
I was afraid he would turn from me
in mid-flight and see me for what I was.
I was afraid of falling off.

Instead, I married a man whose voice
is brown and crisp as buttered toast
and live in a house the pale gray shade
of a winter sky, the number 10, the letter "O,"
and when we kiss it's all cold water,
colorless against my skin.

Lessons in Kindness

There were just a few at first, colorful—
I let them stay. But in a week the whole
house swarmed with ladybugs, sunning at windows,
prancing across the bathtub. When I saw
one piss on my toothbrush, I lost my cool,
began to slaughter them by the handful.

But I didn't learn. I took a dog instead:
saved him from the pound, scrubbed him, gave him food
from my table. The first time he ran off
I cried, searched the neighborhood. But by the fifth
I'd had enough; the next time he ran
I locked the door. I didn't let him back in.

By the time you came along I'd figured out
how not to sound too interested. I let
you carry on with all your unexpected
acts of kindness: picking up my jacket
from the cleaners, keeping the soap I love
in your bath (though it made you break out in hives),

while I'd show up late for dinner—or forget.
You waited at the bar three hours one night;
it was December, you couldn't start your car
and, of course, I wasn't home. You weren't sore.
"You should've called," was all you said on the phone.
But I was stunned. You never called again.

Once Upon a Time in the West

When you disappeared, I quit the telemarketing firm
to pursue your trail full-time, scanning the highway
for signs of where your lips and hands had gone,
retracing our last road trip: the hot unvegetated drive
from Houston to El Paso, the fingernail clippings
you slipped out the window, the sweat sucked
from your pores in the air around Luling and Comfort—

the Love's Truck Stop an hour out of San Antonio
where the car overheated and we spent the night
making love at the dark end of the parking lot;
the Mexican dive near Ft. Stockton
where we stopped for lunch, beer and burritos.
The young Puerto Rican waitress
(I learned on my fifth trip through town)
finished school and went to work for a law firm.
But otherwise it's the same, each taco echoing
the shape of your half smile, mouth full of food.

Always I am closing in, you are just
a few miles ahead, at the next gas station, beyond
the rock formation rising on the horizon—
when I turn on the car, the soundtrack you left behind,
weird harmonica repeating, a sign
for the wronged man, the hero who gets his revenge:
one bad guy's death to take back
a brother swinging from a rope, decades of guilt.
You are the almost satisfied hero riding off straight
across the desert, not stopping to look back.
I am the audience left in the dark theater,
teeth slightly parted in longing with no way
to call you back, to tell you it is not enough.
I will push the repeat button until my thumb goes numb.
I will hear that song again.

Parts of Speech

Tomorrow, I will build a universe
of ink and write you subject to my pen,
controlling all you do and think in verse
and changing every loss of mine to win;
for instance, I could start with adjectives,
crossing out the *old* that I've become,
replacing *dull* with *lovely*, or I'd give
your *careless* words a turn to *grateful* ones.
And then for nouns—inscribe your *apathy*
as *care* with but a movement of my wrist,
to trade distaste for passion, transform *me*
into *she*, and thus by you as her be kissed.
Or better than this wordy love-retrieving
I'll simply stop all verbs, keep you from leaving.

After We Called It Quits

My shrink told me to take some time for myself
and recommended yoga. But rolling around on mats
breathing heavily was too much like sex without the payoff.
After getting stuck in the triangle pose,
feet spread wide, inner thighs aching like sin,
I was too mortified, too much in pain to go back.

I enrolled in an astrophysics class at the local
university to distract myself with star formation.
The violent story of universal birth, the matter
and antimatter pushing against each other,
letting nothing else survive for billions of years;
how could I not think of you?

Desperate, I went to the psychic down the street.
She offered a potion to bring me face to face with love.
But then what? Eventually, the universe would settle,
matter fanning out into suns and galaxies, antimatter shrinking
back: the black holes that hold it all together. Like most men,
you wanted children and someone to do the laundry.

I was sick of being the anti. I chickened out and only
pretended to drink, then told the psychic her potion
brought me herself, for indeed she was standing before me.
We got together, had dogs instead of children,
and wrote a book on coping in a contemporary universe.
It's not a love story; it has sold well.

That Kind

On hungry days, I sleep with men
for meals: I always stay the night.

In the morning, after he leaves for work,
my routine prowl through kitchen cabinets

and refrigerators for something pleasurable
but not too obvious, something he'll not

miss when he comes home: toast with jelly
smeared across its hard surface, noodles dripping

with melted butter, a slice of ham or turkey
salty on my tongue, olives, round and cold,

a glass of juice thick with pulp (I always
wash the glass out carefully, put it back

in its exact spot). Never eggs or avocados.
Never things that might be counted.

Once I went out with a man who kept
smoked salmon and brie in his fridge,

the pink tender flesh of the fish, the soft
rich cheese giving between my lips—

too good to pass up; I finished them off.
But I'll never see him again. I'm not that kind of girl.

For My American Lover, Upon My Leaving

The first time I walked into an American
supermarket I nearly fainted, right between
the isles of bread stacked above my head,
beyond my reach: brown bread, flat bread,
big puffy bread, tiny bread like fists,
bread long and thin as arms, bread
with nuts on top, bread with fruits inside,
so much bread it overwhelmed the shelves,
threatened to burst onto the floor.

At home, the store shelves were empty—no
butter, no cheese, no meat, perhaps a few
expensive cans of mushrooms or a box
of Dutch milk only foreigners could afford.
I had to wait in line for a loaf of bread.
Most days they'd run out before my turn to buy.

You had never gone home empty-handed;
how could I explain my first taste of *freedom*—
not saying anything I wanted without fear
the nosy neighbor would report me to the authorities,
but bread I could buy and waste at will.
You wouldn't understand the phrase *too much*,
but I had learned to live with hunger.
What was I to do with all of your affection?
Squander it, buy it up in boxes for fear
one day your shelves, too, would run empty?

Sofia in April, 1997

Amid dull puffs of smoke
from engines and filter-less cigarettes,
the thick gray noise of people and trains
arriving, departing, pushing off
toward some distant countryside
that amounts only to more of the same:
bread lines an hour long,
holes sewn, a third time, in worn-out socks,
and a gray sky that hangs like an old shirt,
refuses to storm or clear off, just hangs—

upon the platform where a train
arrives from Vratza, two small boys emerge
in clean white shirts and matching pants,
trailing a father like proud birds.
The older grips a sprig of daisies
half bent, the tendrils curled
around his fingers: small hope.
But for the woman who will step
off the train, take the flowers carefully
like precious crystal, lift
the boys in her arms, each in turn,
whisper how she missed them: home.

Atlas

Vast landscapes fit neatly on my shelf
and Phoenix is not so far away
from Statesboro, Georgia, where I sit,
the thin paper unfolded in my lap. Even Tokyo
with its colorful kimonos and fat men
wrestling in their underwear is in arm's
reach on a map with the right scale.

I move across to Cairo while the baby sleeps:
pyramids and bones cocooned in rotting fabric—
sometimes even the fetuses were preserved.
I imagine wearing a blue headscarf in the brown
Sahara, carrying the baby in my arms,
dwarfed in those giant triangular shadows;
or I shift her onto my hip to buy
a live chicken in the marketplace,
pushing my way through crowds of turbaned men.

I know I will never visit Siberia or confront
snow drifts taller than my house,
though I can see the white crystals piling
in its outline on the map and recall the fur hats
they wore in Dr. Zhivago. Novosibirsk is only
a mark on paper I can fold away when I go
to the climate-controlled grocery store
where the people dress like me and the chickens
are plucked clean and wrapped in plastic,
their skin pale pink and bloodless.
They sleep as peacefully in their refrigerated pose
as the outlined continents and oceans.

Leaving the Dig

He taught me history, how to finger
strips of cloth and stone,
piecing their lives together—
long days by the river
leading the sheep to drink
or washing thick wool in biting water,
hands growing stiff with cold—
filling in gaps like the ceramic pots
in his collection, colorful segments
embedded in a mold of plain clay
to show what the whole might have been.

He spent months jotting down
what bits of song the grandparents could recall:
a man imprisoned so long
the clothes have rotted on his body;
a girl who begs her beloved
to cut off her head with a saber.
"We don't even know her name," he whispered,
the mystery meaning desire.
It's true, I thought, *she has escaped.*

All night on the other side of the tent
I imagined making love to her,
felt her goat-milk breath on my neck
and fingered the long scar below her jaw—
I wanted to be caught by that river's current
like so many shards and pieces of cloth,
dumped in an oblivion of ocean.
In the morning I ripped the penciled notes
from his book, the marks smudged
like a kindergartener's exercise,
and set off west, my shadow
spreading out in front of me,
earth's only mention of my presence.

A Fairy Tale

What girl could resist the need to believe,
Plato's lost halves reunited
in that "he makes me feel complete"
all the glassy-eyed brides ooze
on *A Wedding Story*?
I'd dream about you over breakfast,
and glow when you sent me mums at work.

Soon, I'd plastered myself
into domestic paradise;
you finished the dishes after chicken Florentine
while I ran to pick up milk or drop off
the rented movie from the night before.
Saturdays, we trimmed
hedges and pulled up weeds,
our faces smudged with soil
later scrubbed pink
and smiling at dinner parties.

I even began to iron shirts for you,
pressing hot metal hard
against the starched and flattened fabric,
moving carefully between buttons,
reinforcing creases,
passing over and over,
burning like the days
into our flesh.

Portrait: Girl at 19

My mother's always running on about life—
it's tough, not fair, too short, what you make
of it—words bounce from her mouth like a reflex.
She's trying to give me some advice without
having to get too much involved,
hoping I'll imagine what I haven't lived—
like when she said "Life's not all black and white."
I thought of old photos, her growing up.
She knew what she could not do, got married
to have sex, then got divorced. And though
she noticed something wrong and said *you know
you can talk to me*, I couldn't. What I did,
I did alone. Sure, I thought of those films
from Catholic school, where the women sat—
a single white light behind them to shade
their faces black—and spoke of disgust, regret.
But what I felt was not disgust.
Instead, I recalled the trip back from the coast.
We headed west all afternoon, the sun
burning through the windshield. My mother's face
was lit—so white I couldn't see its features
as she stared ahead at the road, and when
she turned to speak to me, her face fell half
into black shadow, and I was afraid
of that sun's piercing anger, afraid it would burn
through glass. So when it finally gave in,
yielded to soft pink and orange, what I felt
was not sin, even though I bled for weeks.
It was the sigh of relief that spread
across the sky and reddened the horizon.

Stolen Child

The night tricked me. The stars in the window
glinted like broken glass and I believed
for a moment that grief had broken through.

It wasn't true. The air was unmoved,
pressing down against my wrists as it has
every moment since they stole him from his bed—

it was my fault, so sound asleep I was
I did not detect their wolf scent and they tore
from him every bit of flesh, like roses

in early morning, hardly bloomed before
they're cut and ground into perfume.
I don't wish for the tug of his fat finger,

the tunelessness of his songs. I don't assume
he'd be better off here than in the dirt.
What I wish is that he never felt the claim

of their yellowed teeth spreading him apart,
the air closing his mouth as he tried to blurt
my name, the stars blinking down like strangers
having never been mothers.

The Lost Mommy

We lost mommy again, looked for her everywhere, first the obvious places: under the tables, sofa, behind the bed, in the kitchen cabinets, out in the flowers, under the bushes. You lost your mommy again, the neighbors said when they saw us searching. We waved and went on playing, enjoying our motherless state for a few hours, taking off our shoes and jackets, running barefoot in the leaves. But then it began to grow dark, and still no sign of her yellow hair and white teeth. The dogs came by to sniff—don't pee on our mommy, please, we said, hoping she was in the tall grass, among the large tree roots, somewhere we'd missed.

The birds stopped singing and went to sleep; the swamps turned from green to black, and still nothing. Who will sing us to sleep? Who will read us our bedtime story about the lost children whose mother searched everywhere for them? No, actually it was the father who searched, their mother was a witch. "Maybe we should get a new one," said the littlest. "We could try the forest," said another, "like in the book, the house made of candy." "Tomorrow," said the oldest. "It's time to sleep." We went inside to find the story and out fell mommy, slipped from between the pages. "Where were you?" we said. "Fighting that witch, your mother, all day," she said. She was bent a little around the ankles and wrists and her hair was wrinkled, but she was there, and she was ours. We held on tight until our fists ached and our fingernails pinched under her skin. We wouldn't let her go again.

II.

II

Letter in Response to a Friend's Suicide Note

250,000 people live off garbage
in the capital city of Mexico,
right across the border, so far away
it might as well be another planet.

You are collapsed against the cheap
motel carpeting in the suburbs of Atlanta
no longer breathing in the residue
of semen and cigarette ash.

A few minutes ago you wrote
a few angry lines with the hotel pen,
your last words running into the hotel logo,
not enough to do anyone any good.

A woman in a Cairo prison wrote her memoirs
on toilet paper with an eyeliner smuggled to her
by a prostitute, the makeup smudging
against the soft tissue, blurred but barely readable.

She said *then, when I began to write,
there was no more prison. When I began to write*

What if I could tell you I loved you once
and you never knew, I was afraid to say it
and I could not look you in the eyes,
you seemed so far away and so close.

I want to say keep the pen pressed to the page
until the hotel walls fade and you find yourself
out amid the warm night air. Come closer,
tell us more, tell us why we love.

Street Dogs

If it's true that dogs are reborn souls of suicides,
then what seem mere shadows haunting garbage heaps

become recognizable, skin stretched around the nose
and jaw, teeth sharpened with the unfamiliar instinct

to live. Don't let the narrowed eyes divert you—
the familiar face still lurks behind thick matted fur:

Hemingway asleep atop the Sunday edition,
Dido, trailing an ice-cream-dripping boy,

or L.E. Landon, still wet, just arrived
as one of Ophelia's sixth set of puppies.

Others have grown into humble adults, locked outside
the heated living rooms of comfy chairs where love

is never enough. Better to scavenge, better
to pin your hopes on a carelessly dropped sausage.

A Confession

I must admit that more than once before
I've thought to wrap a rope around my neck,
to chase the busy tide too far from shore,
or, like my cousin Jude who fell—a fleck
of dirt—off a cliff in Butte, Montana
(I knew from how my mother said the word
accident what really happened), plan a
last dive, pushing through air, a heavy bird.
But what keeps my feet from kicking out the chair
or lifting off the ledge is that one moment,
half way to ground and half way out of air,
when the world might backspace, unindent,
reveal the wonder I long ago forgot
too late to climb back up or cut the knot.

The One That Got Away

The dead remind me of you,
road-side—
not the regular
squirrels and possums,
but those large and beautiful—

like that deer we saw
on our way to Memphis,
its graceful limbs bent so awkwardly
you couldn't drive
anymore that day,

or the moose
that summer in Yellowstone,
its eyes already
chewed out by flies.
I don't think you ate
for the rest of the week.

Strange, you'd said, such life
wasted on a fender.
I saw you then
bolting through the wild shade,
weightless on the delicate moss.

I imagine you now, running
straight into the sunlight of an interstate,
refusing to stop
for the pavement.
The car that hits you is in a ditch,
its hood bent by your still
magnificent antlers.

Entropy

One emerged high in the Alps, an imposing
August sun thoughtlessly exposing
his eight-thousand-year slumber under ice.
The hair was well intact, complete with lice,
and his clothing—a waterproof grass kilt
frozen before it could begin to wilt—
clung modestly to his hips. A quiver
of arrows, an unfinished bow, a sliver
of a dried mushroom—even his last meal
of einkorn, undigested, will reveal
secrets we are dying to know.
                              Another, found
in Siberia, a block of ice locked around
her flesh, preserving her two-foot feather hat,
leather boots, blue and green tattoos, blonde plat,
each fingernail, each cell a miracle
unbothered by time or changing fashion,
reminding us all of our great passion
to be crystallized at death's moment,
to freeze the universe, forever prevent
wrinkles. To wake to perfect muscle tone
after sleeping through so much civilization.

Cadaver Room

The stainless silver tables,
cement floor with its hoses and drains.
No one likes a mess.

I say cadaver. I see body,
a tattoo of a foreign word on her left ankle,
six piercings in her ear
(the earrings have been removed).

We cut against the muscles, forcing our way
through the vast forests of bronchioles,
the cave of a heart, stiff and thick as a tire.
Try to sort out the thin tubes
of her ovaries and all her unborn children.

Did she spend her nights alone?
Share a small apartment with a man who took
her earlobe and all its metal into his mouth?
With a woman whose tongue covered
the sign on her ankle like a blanket?

I trace its outline into my notes
and look it up later. It's Chinese.
It means *home*, the body, a foot in the door,
a fist in the mouth, the long slow sex after lunch.
But she no longer needs the lie:

cadaver, an empty house and all its furnishings
left behind for us to rumble through,
plunging our scalpels deeper
than her lovers ever dared.

Grandmother's Machine

The needle's eye was clear as a teardrop
she could no longer see;
pushing the small white tip through
was my job,
click click of the machine singing
daisy, daisy, tiny dresses for my dolls,
thread between her teeth,
feet working the pedal.
Thick black-rimmed glasses
sliding down the tip of her nose.
I wore them around the house once;
they made the cheap carpet warp
like the inside of a bowl, singing
I'm half-crazy
cutting loose the threads
all for the love
sun cutting through the windows,
smoothing down the small creases,
the seams in my hair,
her thickened fingers
tap tapping to the rhythm.

She left me the machine
but you'll look sweet
I wanted the glasses
upon the seat
I wanted the sun cutting the threads,
rough fingers smoothing the seams,
voice cracking on the high notes
of a bicycle built for two

Grandfather and Dog

I stood beside the hole, looked up at him,
waited. At Grandma's funeral he'd cried
but now his eyes just stared, detached and dim,
and soon the dirt flung was enough to hide
the lifeless form. The early evening shadows
defined his wrinkles, and I saw the sweat
drip off his clenched jaw, but only God knows
what he whispered through his cigarette.
I heard that after Grandma died, his dog ate
with him at the table; he read her all Scott's
novels, and later, my mother would relate
how he'd kept the dog alive with morphine shots
as though he knew he could not go on alone—
the hole I stood by six months later was his own.

Love and the National Defense

If love were a dirty bomb, you could set
it off in Washington and it would spread
into the suburbs unseen, contaminate
the air and water. People would breathe it, feed

on it unknowingly and slowly love
would infiltrate their lungs, make their fingers burn.
In a week, you'd see them start to pair up, leave
the office early for lunch and not return;

even the evangelists are born again—
this time to love—they grab the nearest nun,
and scientists are too involved to look
for cures, not that anyone cares. *Attack*

on US, the foreign press reports
with real concern, seeing the SUVs
abandoned on the interstates, the airports
unguarded, army generals on their knees.

Don't they know love is always like that,
tearing you out of the spaces you once thought
meant something, making you forget each
last defense, the guns rusting along the beach.

A Personal History

On September 6, 1944,
the Russians crossed our border in the north.
Of course, it'd been decided long before:
twenty-seven million dead should be worth
something, Stalin said, and walked away
from Potsdam and Tehran with the biggest shard
of Europe's broken glass, much to the dismay
of my father, whom the Party barred
on account of his Sorbonne education.

But his disgust never turned to anger,
except one New Year's Eve—every station
broadcast at midnight the routine languor
of Zhivcov's national address, the face
sneering on the new TV that took thirteen
months of his salary to buy. The space
of tension, then the shattering of the screen
as my father threw the champagne bottle straight
into the man's teeth. The glass wound, severe,
sparked and fizzed. My father, no longer irate,
turned slowly, raised his toast to the New Year.

Democracy Comes to the Black Sea

We are all topless, men, women, children
exposed, flaunting freedom like pink-breasted birds.
We talk loudly, crammed upon the sand,
can't breathe from all the cigarette smoke,
can't feel the wind for the barricades
of plastic floats, portable radios, and beach chairs
we have learned quickly to consume.
We let the water lap no further than our waists,
the transparent water that goes on forever.

Years ago we looked out and saw the west—
one swimmer could pass unnoticed, break
for the far shore. We weren't worried
about the undertow, only the need to make it
out to the edge of the horizon, looking back
on the rows of red and yellow umbrellas,
the hot swarming bodies shrinking
into a single mass of flesh. Now there is nothing
to escape, nowhere left to go. Now we sit
and burn, naked to the world, finding nothing:
not freedom, not release, only the sun's heat.

Deserts at Night

I turn over, shoulder hitting the mattress hard.
Too much to drink again. I need a glass of water
but it's cold downstairs so I stay in bed
and think of deserts stretching out as far

as I can see in all directions, like my bed.
Empty but for me, it seems to be expanding
though not as rapidly as the desert
which grows every year by the size of Vermont—

sand rolling over grass and shrubs, covering
farms and towns like ancient tombs, pushing back
the blue expanse of ocean and leaving white—
dust and salt flats forever. All this talk

about meteors and aliens when the narrative
of catastrophe is so close: as many grains
of sand as stars. They chafe against each other
as they cross the globe, wailing like demons.

I've thought of building walls to keep the dunes
back, shoveling out the sand where it drifts
over doorways, seeps through slits
in the window casing; but it's pointless.

At night the desert grows cool and across
the wrinkles of sand the moon's blue light
casts a shadow like the current of the ocean
rippling out forever beneath my feet.

Postcards From the Field

No roads.
It took us weeks
to get here, the sand dunes
kept shifting and our dollars meant
nothing.

Teshit—
the driest place
on earth. It rains once in
a decade, and rain will cause more
harm than

good, stir
the infertile
ground with stains of life, rouse
the locusts. Weeks ago, it rained.
Now fear

has come
to those of us
who read the danger in
their changed color, have seen the sun
go dark.

When you
touched me I felt
a thirst rising like sand
between my lips, desert I could
never

cross; now
the thunder sets in;
I drink you like the rain.
When the locusts come they will leave
nothing.

Playing the Rain

It was raining
and it was going
to rain, that was my life—
dodging into underpasses,
thinning myself against
the sides of buildings,

up under rooftops of buildings
where it wasn't raining
as hard, my shirt wet against
my skin, shoes going
squish with water that passes
for life but is not life.

If I had a different life
that well-lit building
would be home, I'd pass
inside out of the rain
and I wouldn't be going
anywhere else against

my will, against
my better judgment. But this life
was my life and going
nowhere but the next building.
Once, to avoid the rain
I ran into a warehouse that passed

for an arcade and passed
three hours fighting against
the evil army and reigning
T-virus (to save what little life
was left), stalking vacant buildings
not knowing where I was going—

I was never going
to win; I couldn't even pass
the first level—the buildings
kept yielding zombies against
me—a quarter for each life—
but I kept playing, the rain

pounding against the building
as I died, passed back into life
again, and the rain kept going.

III.

Wild Child

We wanted rain, prayed for rain. But it rained for three months, the floods reached up and washed our city into the ocean—we had to move inland where a new coast had formed.

One day, a small child's head appeared out past the breakers, bobbing like a black buoy. Soon, he began swimming to shore, coming up from the deep waters of the ocean, naked and white as foam. He played about our doorstep, finding leaves and pine cones, small sticks to entertain himself, quiet as the water had made us all. My husband shooed him off like a mosquito, but I felt like a mother. It was not charity. I wanted to go to him, hold him, tell him, you don't have to go back to the cold sea, you can stay here with us, our freshly painted house, and we will love you. But he was wild as the water—and I was afraid.

The day I saw the jellyfish wrap around his leg, the sharks slowly circling as he cried out—the first sound I ever heard him make—I took the boat out, pulled him aboard, dried him in my clean towel and said don't be afraid, you will live with us now. His bare feet sloshing through the living room until the floorboards sank, his black hair flashing like a wave against the bookshelves, soaking the thousands of unread lines, all the theories we had based our lives on, my husband glaring at me from the side of his mouth saying *what have you done,* saying *it's too late your motherhood will ruin us all.*

First Child

They were prepared for the event, the iron
gate swinging its rusted hinges open

to the Great Flood, and all the animals two
by two on the stupid wooden boat. True.

But no one ever tells the story's after,
the dailyness they met once the disaster

dried up, the dishes ground into the mud,
the stuffed dogs with ears torn off, how they tried

to air out the oriental rugs
and antique curve-legged sofa (minus legs)

but found them stained with water marks and mildew,
their previous state unreturnable to.

What is ahead is scarier than forty days
of rain, a dark that licks against the face

until you can't see ahead but can't go back—
the cave is longer than a life. No mistake.

Better sit on the top, shove closed the door,
return the world to what it was before.

Learning the Language

Da da
testing sounds out
brr brr louder filling
the house, ba ya ya, his small mouth
open

then closed,
ma for mommy,
ma for I'm so tired,
for when will they know what I mean,
hey yey?

She hears
his sounds crowding
the air like concrete stairs
that will not collapse when stepped on,
promise

of sense,
ah mm, if he
can just manage to get
them all together in the right
order.

When she
opens her mouth
words flutter easily
about like piles of thin papers.
Mommy,

cracker,
all the things he
wants. But was there ever
a time she knew what she wanted?
When she

says love
the steps crumble
into broken mortar
and rocks. No one is home, they've long
moved on

and left
no note behind,
no scrawled-out number, no
map to find them nor plans for how
to build.

At the Window

Propped on the bulging couch in the front room,
our foreheads pressed against the glass,
we watch the trees pull back their shadows,
the squirrels flip their tails at a twig,
all business.

He stretches his stumpy legs to see a dog stop,
sniff, squat on a small tuft of clover;
women in bright red head scarves pushing strollers;
Jehovah's Witnesses with purple fliers.
No one notices us.

The radio plays so quietly all we hear are bits of a song,
a woman's voice, sunlight on our skin a thin blanket.
I don't need anything else, she sings,
or did she?

We don't hear the clock, silent on the wall behind us,
its hands like little dervishes unwinding the threads
from our fingers, unspinning the hours
from our days.

Before Language

We walk the streets, pulling leaves from the trees,
petals from the flowers.
They wouldn't last but now
the net of the day catches them,
pins them in the albums with the photos
we will never show to anyone.
The clouds pass over us like words
we might one day say to one another;
we have no use for them.

When it rains, we pull the letters off the shelf,
wear them on our heads,
an *o* around the ankle, *d* tucked behind an ear,
g pinching the bridge of a nose.
They hang there as though
their only purpose were adornment.

At Eight Months

The world is calling you,
its pink pigs with squeaking noses,
circus animals hung from strings,
bells and plastic lids
and spoons for banging.

The world is calling
with its coffee tables and swivel chairs,
chairs that slide away
when you reach for them
or fall on top of you when you push too hard.

With its bare feet in summer,
mosquitoes that bite,
and hurricanes downgraded to tropical storms
carrying your inflatable swimming pool off
to god knows where;

and when the family dog
you were sure was your friend
turns and bites your hand
sick of you pulling at her fur,
you wriggle out of my arms and go back for more.

Already you have learned to open and close
your fat hand, holding it in the air,
waving goodbye.

First Words

Not mama, dada, baby, but ball.
Then big ball, blue ball, soff ball,
sounds from the hard life of objects,
sounds he can open and shut at will.

Not like people who come and go,
sunlight ducking behind a cloud,
crackers disappearing in a mouth.
Balls can be thrown, kicked, held.

He controls the language of balls,
the bounce and roll. Ball: an apple in a dish,
a round wood box full of Mommy's earrings,
a globe floating on its metal axis.

He grabs the fruit and throws it on the floor,
juice spattering the tile.
He breaks the wood box into splinters,
scattering the earrings, unmatchable pairs.

Takes the earth, light and hollow,
too big to reach his arms around,
slams it into my leg,
rolls it across the floor.

After Breakfast

Foot in my mouth, finger in my nose,
prying me open for a peek, what's it like in there?

then on to the chairs, sofa, dangerous horse
with wheels. I say be careful, don't fall.

He pauses a moment then goes on
throwing thick legs up and over.

Now there's a block pounding my chest,
a ball thudding against my head,

little warrior in a diaper: how he will take
and take, how he will unscrew

things he cannot screw back,
pull the world apart to see what it looks like,

basket after basket of toys sloshed across the floor,
the cup he grabs from my hands

to anoint himself in cold coffee,
surprised at the wetness, new baptizer.

I would ask for a moment of silence
but silence is a sign something is wrong,

a roll of toilet paper spread
like new snow across the Persian rug

photos of great-grandparents torn
like puzzle pieces around the empty albums.

I remember how I used to take breakfast
alone on the porch with a novel

I would finish before dark, its heroes
brushing painlessly against my fingers.

Late Afternoon

Grass bows its blades,
branches wave their leaves,
the sky blinks its fat blue eye.
He laughs at the sky, laughs at me,
pulls the daisies up by the roots,
my boy, my sharp little arrow.
Even the moon has stopped
to watch us pass the yards, the cars,

nearing the shops filled
with expensive wooden toys,
fancy chocolate hearts.
We pause at the shoe store window
where the bright red sneakers we can't afford
gleam like a smile behind the glass,
then head into the drug store
for red finger-paint shaped like a heart.

On the way home a dark cloud
rises at our backs, leaving a gap
where the sunbeams seep through:
it will spill the rain down on us like spears.
We hurry home, paint our feet bright red
and dance in the driveway
before the rain washes the paint away,
before it runs down the sidewalk
the pale pink shade of his skin.

How the Earth Lost Its Moon

He stabs his stick into the sky,
spears a small white puff.

The cloud bleeds,
runs down the stick like rain—

look, I got a cloud down—
but it dries in the heat.

So he spears the moon,
look I got the moon,

holding it in his small fist.
His stick has pierced a hole

all the way through.
Here, he says, *I got it for you.*

This is before he knows anything
of sonatas or poetry,

of seduction or pain
(it is always a matter of pain

for someone)
before he thinks to ask

whether I want it at all
but I take it

as though it were a game.
It is wet and cold as a dog's nose;

I have no use for it.
It slips through my fingers

like albumen, spreads
across the grass, an eerie glow,

all that is left of the goddess,
gone after the next hard rain.

Art Lesson

The boy draws the sea so mommy can swim:
here Mommy, he says, *swim*.

I hold the sea up to the light,
the pitchforks of his waves cutting my hands.

I tell him where to draw the red lines of blood
here, and here where it hurts.

He jabs his marker into the paper
not knowing that where the blue

bleeds through it leaves spots on the table,
doesn't stop with one page, with two.

It's the world, he says, the continents
jutting out of the awkward circle.

He signs his name, *K* leaning
as though it will topple,

its sharp edges knocking into the planet,
unaware of how men sign their names to slaughter:

Endlösung, *Directorium Inquisitorum*,
the worst kind of torture.

Even war begins on paper, a long-named resolution
blocking up the desks of dignitaries

before it empties its bullets and flutters off
pinning us all, wingless.

You can have it, he says, letting the pages
slip to the floor, markers drying on the table.

We rise from our chairs,
step over the earth, walk on his sea.

Clothes for Iraqi Orphans

Our good deed for the season: my son's old clothes
piled in plastic bags to be sent to the orphans in Iraq.

No longer needed and practically new
(like the young dead) in search of a body.

How American, at Christmas, to send clothes
as though they could offer healing

or embody love, the same way grandparents
who live far away send too many presents.

I want to write, *I'm sorry*, across the small tags,
I'm sorry we killed your mother, your father.

I want to send my grief in the bags instead of clothes,
I want it to hold those small bodies like the mother lost.

I want it to be as large as the bags, the weight
we must carry with us, struggling to balance

when one child owns enough socks for ten, when one
sleeps quietly to the hum of an air conditioner,

another's hot sleep broken by the crack of bombs,
waking to wonder will this be it, the last time.

And what, I think, if the children have lost limbs?
What if there's only one leg, what will they do

with the spare shoe? Find another child who has lost
the opposite foot? I think of marring the clothing,

cutting off a shirt sleeve, tying knots
in one leg of each pair of pants

as a sign of the damaged lives, as a sign
that I know better. But I don't.

I send the clothes neatly folded, clean,
the way every child deserves to be dressed.

Housing Nationalization
Bulgaria, 1969

I am only nine. Already
I have seen a dog with no hair,
its body covered in sores
and the vultures circling.

I have seen the streets
stained red with cherries
spilled from the trees,
blackened against the asphalt.

I have seen my own home
turned inside-out, its contents
littering the sidewalk
like the vomit
of some bearded drunk:
sofa, chairs, bookshelves
with the books scattered
open and waiting,

my own smaller bed,
a light rain settling
on the pale yellow sheets,
the pillow ripped open
by a policeman
who thought it might be fun
to do a little damage,
break a few dishes.

The white feathers drift
like cigarette smoke
through the neighborhood.
I chase after them
trying to catch them in my fingers,
trying to push them back
into the open tear.

Dinner With Foreigners

Everything black
on the ride down,
no heat, ice
on the windows three
centimeters thick,
the moon
couldn't get through,
just the click click
swaying against the tracks,
dark consonants beating
into the stiff snow.

After the hugs,
greetings you have carefully
memorized, they try
Clint Eastwood, all
they know of English
and you know
no movies in their language.

You jerk phrases out
like the sweater
you wanted on the train
in the middle of your bag
(your hands stiffening
in the dark cabin)
you got pants, then bra
instead: *Thanks
for invited you
here. The chicken
tastes pretty.*

Conversation clatters on,
you remember
craning your ears
upwards as a child
toward the dark blur

of adult chatter
trying to smile
at the right moments
click click
swaying against the tracks.

Another round of vodka.
One man, an actor
begins to tell a story
with his hands:
the noises of animals,
trains and buses,
you think you understand.
His name is Niko.
You try it now,
just like a game
you played as a girl.

A match flickers
in front of each face
leaning forward,
a string of bright bulbs,
personalities—
you have a personality,
rescued
from the cold dark
cabin of your childhood.

The ride home is ice-free,
lights dim and warm
enough to doze (drunk)
against the soothing
click click click that means
you are moving forward.
And when you remember
the night you remember
how it took place
entirely in your language,
whatever that was.

End of Myth

Hotels are sprouting, white as scars
against the green sides of the mountains,
their signs pointing the way with little arrows—
Hotel Orpheus, Dionysus Inn—
a last reminder of what was here before.
The road still winds like a blind goat but now
it's smooth, all its wounds licked over.
No more sheep blocking up the road,
not a single donkey cart in sight.
My son is disappointed. I told him
there would be horses and chickens,
moos and baas and real livestock smells.
I try to distract him with a billboard
of a cow eating chocolate, but it's no use—
we have those at home, and the signs are clear.
The West is coming, death is banished,
no more toilets made of two foot-platforms
with a dirt hole in the center, steam rising
from its depths like an oracle in early morning.
Everything is ceramic and flushes
at the appropriate moment, carrying away
all mention of your sins. Even the cigarettes
are cleaner, sporting filters and warnings
that they will kill you. We smoke anyway, knowing
it is no longer a matter of life and death.
Only a definition of terms.

The Girl with the Sheep's Heart

When her lover did not return,
she gouged her heart out with a saber
and carried it across the nine hills
and villages to where I was working,
the only doctor for 80 km.
Her mother was furious; to leave
her family behind, her parents
growing old, in need of support,
and for what? For a stupid goatherd
who happened to look striking
in dungarees. What was I to do?
She needed a heart. So we found
a sheep squealing out in the yard,
its throat cut for St. George's Day—
ignorant sheep who had never loved
nor been loved—and put it in her body.
It beat. Now, she is a happy girl.
She brings her mother fresh peaches
in the afternoon and helps her father
tend to the slaughter, blood
of the new goats, arrogant roosters
runs red against her skin.
Believe me when I tell you,
she never sheds as much as a tear.

The Cult of True Womanhood

Jesus the lamb, Prometheus the liver
from whom all things taste finer: give us this day
our daily bread and meat, our stolen fire—
the prayer of a barbecue or flambé
that elevates us above the beastly rare—
and the gods' anger that made rise from clay
a woman, and stuck her in the kitchen, where
bending behind the oven she can't say
she saw them string him on the cross, tear out
his liver; still, she holds a paring knife
to dice the fruit, open the box, discover
the holy ghost is nothing but a vulture.
A prankster, she will teach you how to doubt,
and you will look away, and call her wife.

The Orchard Grower's Wife

It's always about war with men,
always statistics, science and gasoline,
so when the temperature dropped
he chanted *the ammunition is diesel oil,*
digging holes in the dirt to fill with fuel
which ran dry on the third day.
When the wood supplies gave out,
everything that put off heat was set on fire—
furniture and floorboards,
tires taken off an old Volkswagen
rusting behind the well,
the fence he'd spent the three years
of our marriage building up,
and the carved wooden statue,
Lady Godiva on her white horse,
all I had left of my mother.
Why don't you put the baby in, too, I asked,
and I think he would've
if she could have been made to burn like fuel.
The wellbeing of mankind, he said.
I held the baby tight as the fire blistered
Lady Godiva's paint into smoke,
her white horse flaming out across the sunset.

Refugees

The children kept freezing to death;
we buried them in the snow
along the sides of the mountains

which would have been beautiful,
rising like a wolf's teeth to meet us,
famished beneath a new moon.

One son made it, his face chapped
purple, small coughs echoing
through the black cave where we sleep.

He and some other boys
found a rock to kick around
like a ball, but I call him inside:

he will wear holes
in his only pair of shoes
and when we run again, holes in his feet.

Each day the rice pot grows lighter.
His hands burn with fever
swollen as a wolf's paws—

so little joy—and I call him inside,
the rock rolling back down
the steep slope, edge like a tooth opening

to the sky's mouth. He will wear holes
in his only pair of shoes and I call
him in. I keep him alive.

The Fifth War

The fifth war was for the seeds, the right to what was green, and for the soil—more precious than kerosene. Before, the tomatoes had grown thick, wrapping their fingers all the way up the banister, the red fruit hanging like hearts through the summer, you could smell them in every room. We had a secret peach tree that sprouted through the living room floor and the children laughed when the fruit burst orange on their chins, dirtying their shirts. The neighbors saw the stains, soldiers came, dug it up and carried it off. Let it go, I said, but my sister—her two children so young they might never remember seeing a tree at all if she didn't save it—tried to fight them off with a broken floorboard.

Soon after, another armed guard stole the tomatoes. Now, we scavenge, buy what we can on the black market, wild grasses mostly, plant them in a bucket with whatever soil we can get, mixed with old newsprint and asphalt. Place them in the sunlight, pray for the blades to stretch their cells upward, bright yellow turning so green you could imagine whole fields of it, a new skin for every child left in the world.

Notes

"Letter in Response to a Friend's Suicide Note" is written in memory of Chris Kirijan.

"A Personal History": Zhivkov served as the dictator of communist Bulgaria for over thirty years.

"Housing Nationalization: Bulgaria 1969": In communist Bulgaria, it was common for high-ranking Party officials to take houses they wanted away from the families who lived in them.

"End of Myth": The Rhodope Mountain region of Bulgaria, once part of ancient Thrace, is the supposed birthplace of Orpheus and Dionysus.

Acknowledgements

Grateful acknowledgement is made to the publications in which the following poems first appeared:

32 Poems: "Love and the National Defense" in a different version
Calyx: A Journal of Literature by Women: "A Love Poem"
Confrontation Magazine: "After We Called It Quits"
Connecticut Review: "Atlas"
Crab Orchard Review: "For My American Lover, Upon My Leaving"
Cream City Review: "The Lost Mommy"
The Edge City Review: "Grandfather and Dog" and "Entropy"
FOLIO: "End of Myth," "Sorrow and the Empty Sac," and "Synesthete"
The Formalist: "Parts of Speech"
The GSU Review: "The One That Got Away" (published as "Lost") and "A Confession"
The Ledge: "Playing the Rain" and "Letter in Response to a Friend's Suicide Note"
Memorious: "The Fifth War" and "Mara and the Hen"
Mid-American Review: "Wild Child"
New Madrid: "The Woman Who Wanted a Child"
Nimrod International Journal: "Dinner With Foreigners"
Oak Bend Review: "Late Afternoon"
Poet Lore: "Art Lesson"
River Styx: "Street Dogs" and "Lessons in Kindness"
The Southeast Review: "Postcards from the Field"
Southern Poetry Review: "That Kind" (published as "Late Breakfast")

"Parts of Speech" also appeared in *Sonnets: 150 Contemporary Sonnets*, edited by William Baer (University of Evansville Press, 2005)

"A Confession" also appeared in translation in *Literaturen Vestnik* (Sofia, Bulgaria)

Special thanks to all the folks at Washington Writers' Publishing House, particularly Jehanne Dubrow for generously helping to edit this manuscript and Patric Pepper for seeing this book into print.

I would also like to thank all of the poets and teachers who helped shape the poems in this book: Linda Bierds, David Bottoms, James Cummins, Linda Gregerson, Beth Gylys, Leon Stokesbury, C.D. Wright, and especially Don Bogen and John Drury.

Most importantly, I would like to thank my parents Jean and John Feldman for their unfailing support, and my husband Peter and son K.J. for putting up with me through the long process of creating this book.

About the Author

Holly Karapetkova's poetry, prose, and translations from the Bulgarian have appeared in a number of journals and anthologies, including *Crab Orchard Review*, *New Madrid*, *Mid-American Review*, *River Styx*, *150 Contemporary Sonnets*, and the *International Poetry Anthology* (Slovenia). She is the author of over twenty books and graphic stories for children and young adults, including *Goodbye Friends!* and *Knock! Knock!* She also serves as artist in residence and literary advisor for the Rhodope International Theatre Laboratory in Smolyan, Bulgaria, where she teaches, writes, and performs poetry for the stage. She holds a Ph.D. from the University of Cincinnati and an M.F.A. from Georgia State University. She is an Assistant Professor of English at Marymount University and lives in Arlington, Virginia.

Colophon

Text design and layout by Patric Pepper
Cover design by Dimitar Kelbechev

The poems and text are set in Adobe ITC Galliard Standard, which is an adaptation of Matthew Carter's 1978 phototype design for Mergenthaler. Galliard was modeled on the work of Robert Granjon, a sixteenth-century letter cutter, whose typefaces are renowned for their beauty and legibility.

The cover typefaces are Helen BG Thin and Helen BG Light.

This book was printed by Lightning Source, Inc., in the United States of America.

CPSIA information can be obtained at www.ICGtesting.com
Printed in the USA
BVOW08s1930200916

462768BV00001B/57/P

9 780931 846953